Designing Professional Development for Change

A Systemic Approach

James Bellanca

IRI/Skylight Publishing, Inc.
Palatine, IL

The excerpt from *The Leader-Manager* by William Hitt is used with permission of Battelle Press, Columbus, Ohio. Copyright © 1994, Battelle Press.

LB
1731
B445
1995

Designing Professional Development for Change
First Printing

Published by IRI/Skylight Publishing, Inc.
200 East Wood Street, Suite 274
Palatine, IL 60067
800-348-4474, 708-991-6300
FAX 708-991-6420

Creative Director: Robin Fogarty
Managing Editor: Julia Noblitt
Editors: Amy Wolgemuth, Monica Phillips, Sabine Vorkoeper
Book Designer: Bruce Leckie
Formatters: Bruce Leckie, Heidi Ray
Production Coordinator: Maggie Trinkle

Library of Congress Catalog Card Number: 95-75711
Printed in the United States of America.
ISBN 0-932935-94-X

1453-2-95

Table of Contents

Professional Development Defined

"How often do you hear statements to the effect that the continuous professional development of teachers is the key to school improvement? Like so many other single-factor solutions to multifaceted phenomena, the *general* endorsement of inservice education means nothing without an accompanying understanding of *the characteristics of effective as compared with ineffective inservice education efforts.* Nothing has promised so much and has been so frustratingly wasteful as the thousands of workshops and conferences that led to no significant change in practice when the teachers returned to their classrooms" (Fullan, 1991, p. 315).

Years ago, teachers rode in buggies and on horseback to attend annually held "institute days." Back then, reading, writing, and arithmetic, along with geography, state names, and state capitals, were the most important topics to review for annual relicensing. In many cases, institute days, which were necessary to keep teachers one step ahead of their best students, provided teachers with their only "inservice" opportunity.

Today, as educators face the twenty-first century, much more than the annual institute day has changed in continuing education for teachers. Teachers now have multiple options for the content, location, format, incentive, and rationale of their development. Although many school districts still rely on institute days as their primary opportunity for inservice, most have moved to more sophisticated staff development programs. On the cutting edge, however, are those districts that recognize the value of moving staff development into the more productive arena of *professional* development, where staff development becomes a critical tool for promoting constructive educational change.

What is professional development? From the individual's point of view, professional development begins with the individual's election to expand his or her repertoire of knowledge or skills. For a teacher, the means may be a graduate program, workshop, conference, action research project, etc. that helps the individual understand and do higher quality teaching. In the context of this book, however, professional development is not defined from the individual's point of view, but from the *school system's* point of view. From this perspective, *professional development* is a planned, comprehensive, and systemic program designed by the system to improve all school personnel's ability to design, implement, and assess productive change in each individual and in the school organization.

How does professional development differ from traditional staff development programs and inservice? From the system's point of view, *staff development* is the effort to correct teaching deficiencies by providing opportunities to learn new methods of classroom management and instruction, or to "spray paint" the district with hoped-for classroom innovations. *Inservice* is the scheduling of awareness programs, usually of short duration, to inform teachers about new ideas in the field of education, or, in the worst case scenario, to fill mandated institute days with any available topic or speaker. (See Figure 1.)

In many school districts, both terminology and reality overlap. For instance, District A may provide two inservice days at the beginning of the school year, at which teachers assemble to hear "motivational" speakers who are often uninspiring. Every few years, an enterprising principal may bring a graduate course or a three-day summer workshop to the district. In the meantime, the principal may schedule an after-school meeting conducted by a textbook consultant. The end result is that, although teachers hear about new ideas, they rarely receive the support to use them well.

District B is more serious about staff development. During its September and February institute days, principals conduct needs assessments and the central office's staff development expert reviews the results. The staff developer then schedules a keynote speaker and adds breakout sessions, and each teacher has a chance to choose workshops of interest. When several teachers at one school tell the staff developer they would like to learn about cooperative learning or a principal asks for an assertive discipline workshop, the staff developer makes the necessary arrangements. Because this person is in charge of the federal funds for the district, he or she also spends time scouting for workshop presenters, arranging for teachers and principals to attend seminars and conferences, and making sure that all funds are spent before the end of the fiscal year.

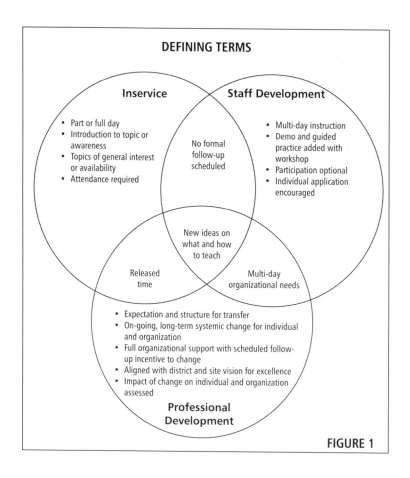

DEFINING TERMS

Inservice

- Part or full day
- Introduction to topic or awareness
- Topics of general interest or availability
- Attendance required

No formal follow-up scheduled

Staff Development

- Multi-day instruction
- Demo and guided practice added with workshop
- Participation optional
- Individual application encouraged

New ideas on what and how to teach

Released time

Multi-day organizational needs

- Expectation and structure for transfer
- On-going, long-term systemic change for individual and organization
- Full organizational support with scheduled follow-up incentive to change
- Aligned with district and site vision for excellence
- Impact of change on individual and organization assessed

Professional Development

FIGURE 1

District C is moving toward a professional development program. Because it is a site-based management district, there is no position labeled "staff developer." The district's assistant superintendent for curriculum and development heads a district-level professional development committee.

As its first action, the committee sends a team of three to be trained as small-group facilitators. At least one facilitator is assigned to each site team. All three facilitators work with the professional development committee to ensure an effective and efficient process.

As its second action, the committee designs a professional development action plan that complements the district's strategic plan. This action plan includes goals, strategies, time lines, and responsibilities for carrying out the professional development committee's five-year "practical vision." This district's vision results in institutionalizing constructive changes in curriculum, instruction, assessment, leadership, support services, and community connections through learning opportunities for all personnel.

As its third action, the committee helps each school site align building plans with performance benchmarks, budgets, and an annual assessment process. Site professional development teams, responding to site needs, identify the site's focus, goals, and actions. They plan for the input of new ideas and schedule follow-up coaching, including an assessment portfolio structure, and determine how each individual can exhibit his or her results to parents and the district. (See Figure 2.) Once per quarter, each site team communicates its progress to the district's professional development team.

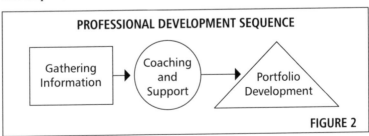

PROFESSIONAL DEVELOPMENT SEQUENCE

Gathering Information → Coaching and Support → Portfolio Development

FIGURE 2

Although the content of each site's plan differs, the structures and processes encouraged by the district facilitator team are very similar. A flow chart of common professional development activities at school sites looks like this:

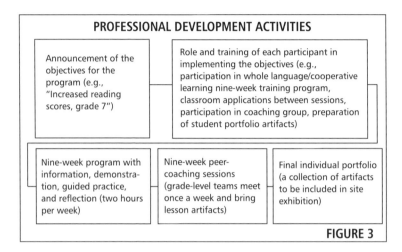

PROFESSIONAL DEVELOPMENT ACTIVITIES

Announcement of the objectives for the program (e.g., "Increased reading scores, grade 7")

Role and training of each participant in implementing the objectives (e.g., participation in whole language/cooperative learning nine-week training program, classroom applications between sessions, participation in coaching group, preparation of student portfolio artifacts)

Nine-week program with information, demonstration, guided practice, and reflection (two hours per week)

Nine-week peer-coaching sessions (grade-level teams meet once a week and bring lesson artifacts)

Final individual portfolio (a collection of artifacts to be included in site exhibition)

FIGURE 3

Although it is possible to argue that the three terms—inservice, staff development, and professional development—are different only in semantics, such an argument would ignore the essential differences between professional development and the other two, as illustrated by the stories of Districts A, B, and C. These differences spring from (a) who makes the continuing education decisions, (b) how these decisions align with the district's agenda for constructive change, (c) responsibility and accountability issues, and (d) the notion of learning for change.

The Evolution of Professional Development

For the most part, movement from the concept of inservice to the understanding of professional development has been an evolution occurring most rapidly in the last decade. As researchers consider what types of continuing education are most effective in helping school districts adapt to the demands for excellence, they rely on practices taken from models of successful school districts, businesses, and industries. A brief look at the history of changes in educators' continuing education will provide a better basis for understanding.

Educating the Educators

Modern inservice education has its roots in the countywide institute days, which provided the only opportunity rural and small-town teachers had to meet their licensing requirements. It was also the only time of the year educators could renew acquaintances with their peers and talk shop. However, as towns began to grow into cities, schools were gathered into districts and systems. In larger systems, management switched from the county seat to city offices. The institute day followed suit. Over the years, other changes followed.

In the late 1950s, the Sputnik revolution caused many changes in classroom curricula. Some of the new curricula required more preparation to teach than a single institute day could provide. Schools encouraged teachers to return to school for additional course work and advanced degrees. Many districts negotiated with professional teacher organizations for "step-and-scale" pay increases as a major incentive for "self-directed" continuing education. This model allowed teachers to receive points or credits that enabled them to jump ahead on the salary scale. The most common formula allotted salary increases for every fifteen hours beyond a bachelor's or master's degree. Today, some districts offer pay-scale steps as high as sixty hours beyond a master's degree.

The most obvious change in educators' continuing education involves the available options for when, where, and from whom they can obtain credits. In addition to annual county inservice and district institute days, single-day, multiday, multiweek, and multiyear programs now provide different time frames for study throughout the calendar year. Likewise, multiple providers from university professors to trainers from intermediate service centers, school districts, private contractors, and federal agencies schedule events and programs at locations ranging from school district offices to mountain retreat centers. The incentives school districts provide for continuing education have also changed. In the "horse-and-buggy" days, the annual inservice was a required school day. Today, most districts provide one to four "student-free" days to allow teachers to learn about new educational ideas. Many districts provide substitutes for teachers and scheduled time for administrators to attend professional conferences or to participate in local two- to five-day in-depth programs. A few districts plan student-released half-days for inservices.

Beyond these efforts, the majority of staff development occurs outside the school day on teachers' or administrators' own time. During this time, educators may attend classes of choice at a local college or university, participate in a district-organized training program, study in a workshop provided by a local museum or teacher center, take a study trip to another country, complete an individual learning contract on the Internet, or work on a district curriculum project.

To compensate teachers for their efforts, school districts provide step-and-scale points for graduate credit, continuing education units (CEU), payment of course and workshop fees, and/or payment of travel expenses for each course completed. Some districts require preapproval so that all course work matches the individual's professional responsibilities; others allow the individual to select whatever professional or personal continuing education event he or she desires.

School districts in the nineties have a multitude of reasons for engaging personnel in continuing education. For some, the main purpose is to motivate and inspire. They seek out inspirational speakers adept at recharging audiences with humor and charisma. For others, it is to introduce ideas that will keep educators informed about new developments in the field. These districts give preference to lectures by learned theoreticians and university researchers. For a third group, the major purpose is to help teachers and administrators master advanced methodology or to deepen their knowledge of curricular content. These teachers, sometimes fortified with coaching, listen to experts, watch mentors model, and practice new approaches. A fourth group uses professional development to plan curriculum and assessment revisions and to bring constructive change into the classroom. In these districts, teachers collaborate for months to design fresh applications and innovative classroom projects.

In every case, the need for teachers to expand their knowledge has become more important than ever. As the information industry continues to grow, the curricula expands and the number of specialty content areas increases. The expanded history curriculum fights for attention with sociology, anthropology, and other social sciences. The science and math curricula grow with every technological advance. Knowledge formerly reserved for colleges and universities is now being pushed into the secondary schools; content saved for the secondary classroom is pushed down to the middle and primary grades. This "push-down" curriculum forces the teachers in lower grades who are unprepared to teach algebra, geometry, physics, and chemistry to return to school. Technology, which in the past was available only to graduate researchers, is now infiltrating even the primary classroom.

Staff Development Programs

It isn't enough for teachers to learn more about *what* they are teaching; they also need to learn more about *how* to teach it. Research on learning bombards teachers and administrators with new information on how children learn and which teaching methods help most. While method fads come and go, advancing research pinpoints the most effective ways to organize curricula, pique student interest, design strategies for authentic learning, and assess student performances.

In the history of education, there has not been a time comparable to the present when professional educators were so readily given substantive information on how to teach matched with what to teach. Beginning in the mid-seventies, this process was propelled by demands for accountability as school districts across the nation combined Madeline Hunter's (1984) work on motivation and instruction with the emerging studies of direct instruction. At the same time, Carol Evertson's (1994) work on classroom management, Raymond Wlodkowski's (1985) insights on student motivation, Sam Kerman's (1979) Teacher Expectations and Student Achievement project (TESA), Bernice McCarthy's (1985) 4MAT Learning Styles, and the Concerns Based Adoption Model emerged as effective staff development programs.

These staff development programs had characteristics that made them different from the inservice events most districts were accustomed to providing on the opening days of the school year or on institute days scattered throughout the school calendar. Instead of one-day "dog-and-pony shows" that featured motivational speakers and relied on "quick-fix" scenarios, these new programs required twenty to thirty hours study of the theory and description of the practice.

In the early eighties, cooperative learning moved to center stage. Robert Slavin (1991) and Roger and David Johnson (1986) conducted numerous training sessions that dealt with their cooperative learning approaches. The Johnsons added training of trainers and other programs to help districts prepare large numbers of teachers in the conceptual model of cooperative learning.

Propelled by the Association for Supervision and Curriculum Development (ASCD), many schools built staff development programs around emerging research that showed the importance of higher-level thinking for all children. Programs such as Feuerstein's (1980) Instrumental Enrichment, Costa's (1991) School as a Home for the Mind, PDK's Impact, NCREL's Strategic Thinking, MCCREL's Tactics for Thinking, and IRI's Patterns for Thinking joined more than two hundred other approaches that provided extended-day thinking-skills programs in a variety of formats.

From Staff Development to Professional Development

At the same time thinking-skills staff development programs were on the rise, other issues began to take districts on different tracks. On one track, questions arose about the weak results of quick-fix inservices and the smorgasbord of staff development programs. The accountability forces in education pushed for clearer and more prescribed outcomes of the time students spent in school. They also pushed for improved management of schools. Staff development began to steer away from teaching methods that might improve learning and moved toward management systems that would ensure raised test scores.

On another track, schools concerned about information overload began to investigate ways for teachers to better integrate the curriculum. Schools on this track formed teacher teams to abandon out-of-date and unrelated curriculum and to connect subject areas through themes and concepts. In many cases, this approach required teachers to spend more time with the content of the curriculum and to develop new ways to assess what and how students were learning.

Each of these tracks utilized new, more systemic ways of organizing teaching and learning. Districts began to have a broader view of staff development. After seeing the results of three studies conducted in the mid-eighties—Joyce and Showers' (1988) study on the importance of peer coaching for ensuring higher application of new teacher skills, Costa and Garmston's (1985) work on cognitive coaching, and the studies of Sarason (1990), Senge (1990), and Fullan (1991) on school change—staff developers began to investigate ways to match personal development with school improvement.

As more schools became familiar with the findings of cognitive psychologists such as Jean Piaget (1972), Lev Vygotsky (1978), and Reuven Feuerstein (1980), they began to understand the concept of systemic staff development. These psychologists, called the "constructiv-ists," challenged the more conventional behavioristic and humanistic theories of learning. The basic tenets of the constructivist beliefs about learning seemed to hold not only for children, but also for adults.

Howard Gardner and his colleagues at Harvard's Project Zero are notable examples of university researchers relying on learning theory as the foundation for implementing more systemic professional development. Starting with Gardner's (1983) theory of multiple intelligences, Project Zero researchers initiated more than a dozen projects in school districts. Their aim was to examine how to introduce learning theory into the classroom. In this way, they hoped to discover how classroom practice and the school organization impacted implementation of the theory.

Michael Fullan (1991) and his colleagues at the University of Toronto provided similar insights from their studies of educational organizations. Fullan's special contributions to the field include his notion of the three phases of change—introduction, implementation, and institutionalization—and the role of the organization in providing the resources, structures, and support, not just for giving information (introduction), but also for helping with the implementation of the new ideas (implementation) and for making new ideas a regular part of the organization (institutionalization).

Most importantly, Fullan should be credited for his leadership in challenging educators to connect personal development to organizational development.

> "Regardless of one's starting point, the evidence is that beginning teachers will get better or worse depending on the schools in which they teach. Continuous development of all teachers is the cornerstone for meaning, improvement and reform. Professional development and school development are intrinsically linked. This means that teacher development depends not only on individuals, but also on the teachers and administrators with whom he or she works" (Fullan, 1991, p. 315).

As a result of these efforts and others, a few leading districts began to change their notions of staff development. Rather than provide isolated staff development experiences designed to "fix" teachers or to change teacher behavior, district leaders began to understand the power of systemic support systems that communicate the idea that learning as a lifelong process is as important for the teachers as it is for the students. The insights into the nature of learning provided by the constructivists have created new issues for the implementation of professional development.

Learning Transfer through Professional Development

In 1992, David Perkins, Robin Fogarty, and John Barell identified the issues involved in transforming staff development into a professional activity. In their work, they explored the process of learning transfer from an *instructional* point of view. From this, they laid the groundwork for an *organizational* point of view.

In the behavioristic model, transfer of learning was seen as impossible. Little boxes were the norm and the reality. On institute days, teachers were exposed to a myriad of isolated topics. During extended training programs, teachers were provided with theories and skills for changing their instructional behaviors, which they were expected to duplicate in their classrooms. In the least professional staff development programs, usually sponsored by textbook companies, teachers were provided with "teacher-proof" activities to replicate in the classroom.

Robin Fogarty (1989) pointed out the weaknesses of this approach. In a research project with thirty secondary teachers, she investigated how the degrees of application varied as teachers learned to teach thinking across the content areas. All were asked to examine teaching from a perspective different from their current practices. Instead of being dispensers of information, they learned to be facilitators who established conditions to promote student thinking and mediators who helped students think more skillfully. As a result, the teachers learned by constructive reflection how they were thinking and discovered how to use what they learned with their students. Fogarty taught by modeling the instructional strategies she wanted the teachers to use. After the teachers had experienced the model lesson, she guided them through reflective analysis that ended with specific classroom plans.

At the end of the forty-five-hour training program, Fogarty observed five of the teachers in their classrooms. After reviewing the observation results, she noted six categories that emerged and labeled them the "birds of transfer." (See Figure 4.)

TEACHER LEVELS OF TRANSFER

Ollie
the Head-in-the-sand Ostrich
OVERLOOKS

Does nothing; unaware of relevance and misses appropriate applications; overlooks intentionally or unintentionally. (Resists)

"Great session, but this won't work with my kids or content" or "I chose not to use __ because..."

Dan
the Drilling Woodpecker
DUPLICATES

Drills and practices exactly as presented; Drill! Drill! Then stops; uses as an activity rather than as a strategy; duplicates. (Copies)

"Could I have a copy of that transparency?"

Laura
the Look-alike Penguin
REPLICATES

Tailors to kids and content, but applies to similar content; all look alike; does not transfer into new situations; replicates. (Differentiates)

"I use the web for every character analysis."

Jonathan
Livingston Seagull
INTEGRATES

Raised consciousness; acute awareness; deliberate refinement; integrates subtly with existing repertoire. (Combines)

"I haven't used any of your ideas, but I'm wording my questions carefully. I've always done this, but I'm doing more of it."

Cathy
the Carrier Pigeon
MAPS

Consciously transfers ideas to various situations, contents; carries strategy as part of available repertoire; maps. (Associates)

"I use the webbing strategy in everything."

Samantha
the Soaring Eagle
INNOVATES

Innovates; flies with an idea; takes it into action beyond the initial conception; creates enhances, invents; risks. (Diverges)

"You have changed my teaching forever. I can never go back to what I used to do. I know too much. I'm too excited."

FIGURE 4

From James Bellanca and Robin Fogarty, *Blueprints for Thinking in the Cooperative Classroom* (Palatine, IL: IRI/Skylight Publishing, 1991), p. 273.

Constructivist theoreticians view learning transfer as the most complex and important element in the learning process. Without transfer either by hugging (an immediate connection within the curriculum) or bridging (a wider connection across the curriculum or into life), learning is incomplete. Thus, transfer cannot be an instructional afterthought or something that just "happens." It must be a consciously planned result of taking *something* (a skill, idea, concept, value, etc.) and moving it *somewhere* (across a lesson, unit, course, job, etc.) by means of a carefully selected *somehow*. (See Figure 5.)

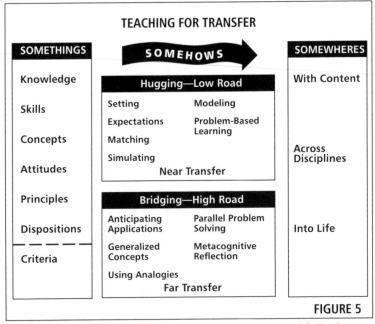

FIGURE 5

From Robin Fogarty, David Perkins, and John Barell, *The Mindful School: How to Teach for Transfer* (Palatine, IL: IRI/Skylight Publishing, 1992), p. 99.

By implication, these constructivist understandings about the process of learning transfer lead beyond what the teacher or trainer does in the classroom. When one considers Fogarty's "birds" in light of Michael Fullan's studies on the new meanings of educational change, it becomes apparent that organizational factors play a major role either in inhibiting transfer or in promoting it. By reversing Fullan's thesis that *there is no organizational change without individual change* to *there is no individual change without organizational change,* the role of transfer theory as the cornerstone of systemic change becomes more apparent.

Transfer Theory in Systemic Reform

In the systemic construct, the notions of organizational change and individual change are woven like a fine rug: pull one thread and you damage the entire piece. Just as the threads in a rug are part of a system, so too are the elements of change in an organization. As the individual constructs new ways to teach from a staff development event, he or she makes changes in the classroom that reflect the changes occurring in the school system. If time schedules, curricular goals, student and teacher evaluations, materials, and expectations remain the same as before the program, there will be little change in the classroom. However, if there is flexibility to change how teachers educate, improvements in the organization and in the classroom will result.

Success with transfer is a double-edged sword. On the one hand, successful transfer is enacted by a learner who gathers new information, integrates the new information with prior knowledge, and ferrets out the best use of the information. On the other hand, successful transfer is enabled by the organizational culture's readiness to accept and promote learning transfer. If the culture is hostile or indifferent to transfer, even the most determined applier of new learning will become frustrated and overwhelmed.

The Key to Change

Learning transfer is the key to individual change and to organizational change. When the adult learner is challenged to abandon reliance on a passive mode of instruction, he or she will discover the joy and the responsibility of intrinsic motivation. At this point, an individual paradigm shift occurs. The learner moves from a passive to an active state of learning. Instead of waiting to receive new ideas and then regurgitate or reject them, the learner takes responsibility for his or her own active mental engagement in the construction of new knowledge. Being aware that the activity requires not only information gathering, but also understanding and application of this information in the classroom, each teacher assumes a professional responsibility for making sure the transfer is successful. Instead of one- to five-day staff development programs designed to "fix" the teacher or administrator or fill in information gaps, professional development programs empower the educator to develop a new understanding and new tools for improving how he or she performs each day on the job.

Consider this example: Roberto, a veteran biology teacher, noticed a growing "me-first" attitude in his advanced placement students. A TV show about science research teams raised his concern about his students' unwillingness to work in groups. After discussing this with his colleagues, he decided to take a course in cooperative learning. He signed up for a five-day, district-sponsored course called "Blueprints for Thinking in the Cooperative Classroom." In addition to the forty-five hours of instruction, he was encouraged to meet once a week for an hour with other teachers in the district. During these meetings, the group planned lessons that incorporated classroom information into their daily lesson plans, reviewed artifacts from previous cooperative learning lessons, built a portfolio of successful teaching experiences, and kept a journal in which they evaluated their own applications and reflected on other ways to improve their use of cooperative learning in the classroom.

Although many of the elements of this example appear quite similar to standard staff development offerings, there are subtle differences. First, Roberto is doing more than just taking a course to gather credit for a step-and-scale pay raise. The credit incentive is there; however, it is given only after Roberto applies the information he gathered in the course. Second, the district created expectations and opportunities to make classroom applications by having weekly peer support sessions. Third, the decision of how to apply what he learned in class was up to Roberto. He had the full responsibility of assessing what he was doing and applying what worked best with his students. Finally, after reflecting on what worked in his classroom, Roberto formed his own understanding of cooperative learning and its place in his teaching repertoire.

When a school district adopts this two-pronged systemic approach to change, the individual *and* the system benefit. In order to mesh system needs with individual needs, the staff developer must shift responsibilities.

The Role of the Professional Developer

In systemic reform, the staff developer becomes a *professional* developer. In this role, assignable to a principal, teacher, or central administrator, the developer serves first to facilitate learning rather than to schedule and arrange events. As a facilitator, the developer tries to promote each teacher's and administrator's professional growth by constructing a plan that empowers his or her colleagues to establish professional-growth goals, identify strategies, assess progress, and construct their own professional understandings of new ideas and methods.

This focus on empowering the individual creates a restructured set of responsibilities for the staff developer. Instead of organizing a smorgasbord of workshops, courses, and events, the developer focuses on modifying the instructional options and the organizational structures. The professional developer becomes an enabler, using a variety of strategies to aid teachers and administrators in the investigation of new learning theories and attendant practices. The professional developer reviews literature on systemic change, especially as it applies to the enhancement of professional educators' knowledge and skills. Then, he or she redesigns the organization's system to fit the new understandings of learning, which accentuates transfer rather than information acquisition. This redesign means not only planning a new professional development system, but also implementing and assessing the system within the context of the entire school.

Regardless of the size or financial status of the district, a professional developer can create a systemic change system. When creating a professional development system that focuses on making constructive changes in teaching and learning, an alignment of transfer practices with district goals that enables all children to learn to their potential is most important. Both poor and prosperous districts can adapt to this model of change—if they are willing.

The most important ingredient in changing from *staff* development to *professional* development is the notion of learning transfer. Understanding the nature of learning transfer and its implications for the development of teachers is essential for the successful development of a program that increases the quantity and the quality of constructive change in a school or district.

Methods of Promoting Learning Transfer

Peer Coaching

There is an increasing number of studies describing the methods of promoting learning transfer. In 1983, Bruce Joyce and Beverly Showers set the foundation for understanding transfer's role in professional development. At that time, they contributed the results of their study on the effects of peer coaching to various models of teaching. In addition to the information they provided on components of peer coaching, they also provided information on the types of instructional planning that seemed to best prepare teachers for peer-coaching work. Their examination of the impact of peer coaching on classrooms supported the argument that when an education program for teachers does not provide a peer-coaching follow-up, the program is a waste of dollars and time. If nothing else, programs without peer coaching produce minimal personal and organizational change.

By implication, Joyce and Showers' (1988) work questioned why any school would spend money on motivational speakers, one-day, one-shot inservices, or quick-fix workshops. Motivational inservice speakers may excite faculty for one day, but, as the chart below shows, without coaching to support implementation, there is minimal change and little lasting effect. (See Figure 6.)

EFFECTS OF STAFF DEVELOPMENT Classroom Application			
	KNOWLEDGE	DEMONSTRATION OF BEHAVIOR	TRANSFER TO WORK SETTING
PRESENTATION OF CONCEPTS AND THEORY	85%	15%	10%
DEMONSTRATION OF BEHAVIOR	85%	18%	10%
LOW-RISK PRACTICE WITH FEEDBACK (MICRO-TEACHING)	85%	80%	15%
COACHING IN WORK SETTING RE: BEHAVIOR AND DECISIONS	90%	90%	80%

Training Strategy

FIGURE 6

Adapted from Bruce Joyce and Beverly Showers, *Student Achievement through Staff Development* (New York: Longman, 1988), p. 71.

Cognitive Mediation

The addition of Art Costa and Bob Garmston's (1985) work on cognitive mediation as the key tool in peer coaching validated and extended Joyce and Showers' studies. Costa and Garmston made a very special contribution when they noted the value of mediated reflection to professional practice. They prepared cognitive coaches to keep the teachers' own thinking at the center of the change universe. As the coaches mediated the teachers' thinking by asking probing, thought-producing questions about theory and practice, the teachers began to manage their learning and direct what changes occured in their classroom practice.

The mediation of cognitive coaching is tied directly to the notion of metacognition. Metacognition, or "thinking about your thinking," was advanced in the early fifties by Reuven Feuerstein, an Israeli cognitive psychologist. In his theory of structured cognitive modifiability, Feuerstein posited how the individual, guided by a skilled mediator's questions that filter distractions from the thinking process, could take control of what and how he or she was thinking. In the mid-seventies, American researchers Palincsar and Brown applied the principles of metacognition to reading practice. In 1991, Robin Fogarty applied the principles to a wide range of instructional approaches, especially in the "nested" model of integrated learning.

With metacognition, the adult teacher or the student learner reflects on his or her thinking processes before, during, and after a task. These reflections, often recorded in a journal or thinking log, are the primary tool the learner has for assessing and refining the performance of a learning task.

Shepherding

The concept of coaching and the practice of cognitive mediation are important ingredients in the "shepherding" that Perkins and Salomon (1988) describe in their studies of learning transfer. According to Perkins and Salomon, the naturalistic and humanistic models of learning thrive on "leaving the sheep alone" to find their own way back to the barn. If transfer happens with this "Bo Peep" approach, it is only because the learner has special talent and commitment to overcome the barriers that prevent transfer. Their studies give preference to the active mediation of learning transfer.

Perkins and Salomon model their approach on the activities of a shepherd. A shepherd points out the best pathways, guides the flock home, and protects it from wolves. In the context of cognitive coaching, a trainer who mediates the thinking process by asking critical questions that challenge the teacher-learner to look at his or her thinking, decision making, and problem solving from new points of view is a good shepherd. This shepherd-mediator points out new paths for thinking through a problem and identifies glitches in application logic. The mediator also structures the sequence of thinking by helping the teacher set goals for learning transfer, monitors the process during the learning experience, and assesses the quality of thinking for the completed transfer. By asking key questions at key moments during the teacher's thinking processes, the mediator empowers the learner to think independently as well as reflect on the quality of his or her own thinking. (See Figure 7.)

SAMPLE QUESTIONS TO MEDIATE THE TRANSFER OF LEARNING

Setting Goals for Transfer

1. What are your specific reasons for learning this material? How do you think you might make use of it in your classroom?
2. Among these reasons, what are your priority goals?
3. How will students benefit from these goals?
4. What are the obstacles to your success in reaching these goals?
5. How will you overcome these obstacles that might block your successful transfer?
6. How will you know you have achieved these goals?

Monitoring Progress

1. How well are you doing in moving toward your goal?
2. How do you know that?
3. What modifications do you think you might need to make? What have you learned that indicates you might change your goal?
4. How will you change your goal?
5. What details have you thought about that will fit with the new goal?

Assessing the Results

1. How successful were you in achieving your transfer goals?
2. What is your evidence?
3. If you did the same applications in the future, what would you change?
4. How would these changes benefit your students?
5. How would you change your thinking processes in the future?
6. What help do you need from me?

FIGURE 7

Systemic Training

Adding to Costa and Garmston's (1985) insights on the effects of coaching and Perkins and Salomon's (1988) studies of learning transfer, Fogarty and Bellanca (1991) examined more systemic training designs that connected supportive follow-up of coaching, the mediative aspects of thinking for transfer, and modifications of school culture. Aided by principals and teachers in a variety of large and small schools, they studied several methods and means that might cause transfer in training to occur more regularly. These studies have produced a number of considerations for what the best practice is for promoting both personal and organizational change through effective professional development designed to produce learning transfer.

If individuals in a school organization are going to transfer learning from a primary learning situation to regular, on-the-job use, expectations for transfer must receive prominent attention. For instance, if a teacher elects to participate in an authentic assessment training program, he or she should know these things from the start:

- He or she is learning the material in order to use it in his or her classroom.
- The training program will provide time and assistance in learning how to put the theory into practice.
- The school system will provide support and opportunities to practice applications of authentic assessment within the daily curriculum.
- The school system will gear its professional development incentives to recognize high-level applications.
- The individual's annual performance assessment will include a major segment for reviewing the applications of authentic assessment in his or her classroom.
- The school system will make a cognitive coach available to assist the teacher in thinking through the application process.

These six components identified by Fogarty and Bellanca are not new. All are found in business training programs and school district professional development efforts that are seeking to increase purposeful transfer. What is unique is the synthesis of these components into a holistic system, which impacts the organization as much as the individual.

Success in Promoting Learning Transfer

Twenty years ago, Malcolm Knowles (1975) identified the ultimate standard for success in adult training programs. He stated that the major difference between adult learners and children is adults' need to engage in learning that has a clear and direct job application. Later studies showed that although adult learners often expressed this need for direct application, employers seldom did anything about it. Peter Senge (1990) advanced this argument by showing that organizations need to design a variety of methods to support transfer of new learning to the job. They must change from assembly-line factories to learning organizations. The school or company that is a learning organization creates the climate for transfer by making structural changes that promote transfer.

In putting these theories into practice, the following examples illustrate what an organization can do to enhance transfer.

I

The training programs conducted by Arthur Anderson Consulting, Inc., at the St. Charles, Illinois, Center for Professional Development have transfer as their primary process goal. Each year, all employees, from first-year recruits to senior partners, come to the St. Charles facility for a two-week training program. All are continually reminded that knowing the content of this intense two-week program improves job performance. In some cases, the program deals with precise accounting procedures; in other cases, complex case studies and collaborative problem-based learning scenarios are emphasized. In all cases, the participants understand that they will be gathering new information, processing it for understanding, and making use of it over the next fifty weeks. On-the-job supervisors and support group colleagues foster a climate for applying the new information. Promotions and future assignments depend on performance assessments that show the individual's high transfer.

II

The elementary schools in Taunton, Massachusetts, have spent the past seven years systemically integrating Instrumental Enrichment, a thinking-skills program created by Reuven Feuerstein. All middle school personnel have received more than ninety hours of formal training in this program. In addition, principals have scheduled time for base groups to review their progress. The director of elementary instructors supervises the implementation of Instrumental Enrichment in three-hour-a-week classroom sessions in grades four through seven. The director also reviews the students' application of thinking skills they have learned.

The Taunton program reflects a learner-centered approach. (See Figure 8.) As many districts do, the Taunton schools support

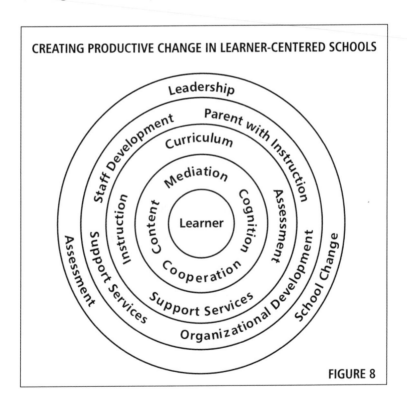

CREATING PRODUCTIVE CHANGE IN LEARNER-CENTERED SCHOOLS

FIGURE 8

the theory that all children can learn. Unlike most other districts, however, Taunton has made a conscious, nine-year effort to put this theory into daily practice through a systemic implementation of the Instrumental Enrichment program.

Teams composed of a classroom teacher, a special education teacher, and/or a bilingual teacher begin each day with an Instrumental Enrichment (IE) curriculum. For the first forty-five minutes, this team mediates students' learning of how to think with specified instruments. During the work stage, students exercise a significant amount of task attention, impulse control, and cooperative interaction. After an IE session, students engage in a traditional basic-skills curriculum. There are several features that stand out in each subject area.

First, the teachers spend most of their time asking questions. Second, questions move from gathering and understanding content to connecting it with the thinking skills stressed earlier in the IE lesson. Seventh graders working with short stories focus on the comparison and contrast skills they learned in IE. Fourth graders who had concentrated on impulse control (stop, think, and make a plan) in an IE session early in the day were later asked how they stopped and planned to solve two-step math problems.

Assessment in Taunton reflects this thinking and problem-solving curriculum. The Taunton district relies on standardized tests to determine how thinking skills affect basic skills. To support this approach, the district has provided intense professional development to fourth- through seventh-grade teachers, principals, and support staff at each of the elementary schools. The professional development program has included forty-five hours of classroom instruction per year for three years and has provided opportunities for peer collaboration, observation, administrative conferencing, model teaching by administrators, and parent meetings, as well as nine years of central office and board financial support.

As a result of rising test scores, the district has developed a plan to expand from elementary schools to high schools. Teacher training and follow-up has begun in the high school in preparation for the introduction of advanced Instrumental Enrichment to all ninth-grade students and their teachers. The assistant superintendent and the director of elementary instruction have been teaching a class of volunteer high school students so teachers can observe the process. Training has also begun for special education teachers in the primary grades. In both instances, the plan calls for initiation of the extensions as well as the introduction of an adult version of IE for parents and community members.

The Components of Learning Transfer

Teaching for transfer calls for a subtle shift in understanding the nature and needs of the adult learner. In the outdated information paradigm that has dominated education at all grade levels since the beginning of the century, teaching and learning are framed by Thorndike's argument (1969) that transfer doesn't exist. According to Thorndike, the individual only has the capacity to take information in and give it back. The knowledge test is the period at the end of Thorndike's sentence. However, when assumptions about learning take on a more constructivist tone in the new paradigm, information is only the first word in the first sentence of a paragraph. Information begins the adult thinking process; application activity, encouraged and supported by an organization's policies and practices, adds to it.

The learning-transfer paradigm calls for a systemic approach to professional development. Instead of one-day, one-shot inservices and a conglomeration of staff development activities, this paradigm creates lifelong learning opportunities for all staff that align with site and district goals. For educators, this constructivist approach to learning has three major components, each of which contributes to transfer to classroom practice: the transfer-promoting organization, the transfer-promoting professional development program, and the transfer-focused design of learning.

However, each of the components, while necessary, is by itself insufficient to ensure the constructive change that comes from putting theory into practice. Working together, they provide the catalyst for a lifetime of learning transfer.

The Transfer-Promoting Organization

The transfer-promoting organization views learning as preparation for life. In this context, its mission charges every school employee to apply the learning theory. All decisions are based on whether or not all children will leave the school better prepared for life in the twenty-first century. Specific goals unite teaching practices with this mission and are the basis for accountability. Consider, for example, the Taunton goals. These five goals are the foundation of decisions made in the district supporting the Instrumental Enrichment program:

- Create lifelong learners
- Develop critical thinking skills
- Enhance all students' achievement
- Create interactive learning environments
- Foster the belief that education is a shared responsibility

To ensure that teachers have the knowledge, skills, and motivation to implement this critical thinking program, the Taunton district, as an organized system, implemented a professional development program to prepare its teachers to meet these goals. Beginning with a small group of volunteers, the district leaders ensured that each middle-grade teacher would receive forty-five hours of classroom preparation in mediated learning. In addition, the district planned time for follow-up coaching, engaged in classroom observation, and requested feedback from the program's trainers.

To ascertain whether the program was taking hold in the classrooms, the district administrator responsible for the program developed a multiple assessment model. First, she looked for regular and consistent application of the program in the classrooms. Second, she traced the changes in test scores. Little change was expected in the first two years of the program, but significant growth was predicted for the third year. To determine whether the district's program would bring about the predicted results, the administrator tracked student performance on the district's basic-skills test and the state's mandated tests. Finally, the administrator looked for other evidence of change. Did student behavior improve? Did referrals to the principal's office decrease? Were there fewer absences? The results were positive, but as in any transfer-promoting organization they did not happen without the planning and commitment of everyone involved.

Organizational Expectations for Lifelong Learning

In a learning organization, formal policies, practices, and procedures make it easy for the district personnel to study new ideas and to take time to implement them. Rather than leave innovation to a few risk-takers, the organization should find ways to encourage all employees to participate in the improvement process. Along with board-approved policies, the administration should post the professional development vision and goals on faculty bulletin boards. They can use the district newsletter to discuss how professional development is a priority and use bulletin boards in each school to help focus all development activity on the vision.

Prescheduled Base Groups

Any individual learning a new theory or practice should participate in weekly base-group sessions. The time and groupings (e.g., grades three through five or subject-alike teachers) should ensure that at least one hour a week is devoted to planning and evaluating new applications. Teachers and support staff should not have to squeeze in this time as an afterthought. In a learning organization, the first learners must be the teachers; therefore, it is an administrative task to make a schedule that provides one hour a week for each group to plan, analyze, and reflect on applications.

The base groups provide mutual support, mediation, and problem solving. To keep members in charge of their own learning, groups follow a planning-assessing cycle that continues week after week. Agreeing upon positive guidelines such as beginning and ending meetings on time, being prepared, listening, and offering encouragement sets the climate for positive support. Consider these examples:

I

Twenty-seven teachers from King Elementary School are in phase two of a program to integrate the curriculum. Working with a district consultant, they have reviewed the ten models of integration. The principal has set multigrade base teams to meet during common planning periods during which each team will select one of the ten models and design a unit for their multiage classrooms. They are expected to bring their design back to the entire group at the next session in one month.

II

Five middle-grade science teachers attended the state conference. Before the conference, they met with the principal and set a goal to find all the information they could about problem-based learning. Each night, the group met to report on the day's discoveries relative to their goal and to select sessions for the next day. When they returned to school, the group met once a week throughout the semester at a time prescheduled by the principal. At the end of the semester, the team presented the principal with a portfolio that included their definition of problem-based learning, lessons they had taught with the model, observations of each other's lessons, and student artifacts.

III

Three high school geometry teachers formed a base group to converse with other geometry teachers via a national bulletin board on the Internet. The department chair scheduled their classes to meet during third period. Each Wednesday, the base group connected to the bulletin board and sent out inquiries for ideas on the unit they were teaching. The members committed to trying one idea per week in class and then reported its effects to the rest of the group.

Prescheduled Cohort Groups

All school faculty should review their applications to see if they align with the school's goals for change. Cohort groups, consisting of five to thirty members and staffed with either a teacher-leader, staff developer, instructional coach, department chair, or site administrator, meet at least three times a quarter to demonstrate or display samples of student work. Most importantly, cohort groups support and celebrate teachers' successes with new applications.

Schoolwide Commitment to Continuous Team Improvement

The school site, John Goodlad tells us, is the locus of change. Peter Senge (1990) argues that team leadership of the change process creates the most synergy. At the school site, it is important that site leadership, whether vested in a principal or a leadership team, recognizes its responsibility for creating a synergy beneficial to all students. For this to occur, leadership must organize productive teams committed to the full implementation of their ideas for change. Such team involvement communicates that schoolwide commitment is not only an administrative responsibility, but a responsibility shared by all. In *The Leader-Manager* (1994), William Hitt describes the characteristics of a well-functioning team.

1. *Common agreement on high expectations for the team.* All members have a will to excel. Principal motivators are high standards, quality, and excellence. Mediocrity simply is not tolerated.

2. *A commitment to common goals.* The goals provide the team members a common focus. All members have a clear understanding of the goals, and they accept them. Further, they realize that the goals can be achieved only through a team effort.

3. *Assumed responsibility for work that must be done.* Each member has a defined job but, in addition, has a commitment to do anything that needs doing. All members of the team have internalized the catch phrase: "If something needs doing, then see to it that it gets done."

4. *Honest and open communication.* The members openly express their thoughts and feelings, and they feel free to ask questions with the confidence that they will receive honest answers. There are no hidden agendas; everything is aboveboard.

5. *Common access to information.* Information is viewed as a vital resource to each member, and it is the leader's responsibility to make certain that every member has the information needed to

get the job done. Except for a few highly sensitive matters, the leader's files are open to all team members.

6. *A climate of trust.* Each team member has an instinctive, unquestioning belief in the other team members. Trust is the glue that holds the group together, and enlightened managers know that trust begets trust.

7. *A general feeling that one can influence what happens.* Members of such a team feel confident that they will be listened to by their leader and that their ideas will be taken into consideration.

8. *Support for decisions that are made.* On key decisions, the affected parties are given an opportunity to express their thoughts and feelings about the matters at hand. The members have confidence in the sincerity of the leader in soliciting their input.

9. *A win-win approach to conflict management.* Both affected parties approach the confrontation with the assumption that each can emerge as a winner. They jointly explore alternative ways in which each party might achieve his or her goals, and how each might help the other achieve his or her goals.

10. *A focus on process as well as results.* On a continuing basis, the team members address these questions: (1) How well are we functioning as a team? (2) What barriers are preventing us from being a productive team? and (3) What should we do to become a more productive team? As a consequence, the team continues to improve.

Practical Vision for Improvement

Synergy is necessary for a well-functioning team to work. School-wide implementation of common goals is a long-term synergistic task that starts with defining the school's ultimate goal. To determine this long-term goal, an annual assessment rubric outlining application standards, short-term goals, and criteria for the school's improvement needs to be created.

The rubric defines expectations for the performances of the individual, the base group, and the cohort group. The rubric also details the strategies and the tools that individuals, teams, and cohort groups should use to gather and weigh assessment data. Individuals' journals, artifacts of student work, lesson designs, and evaluations form the content of the individual's and the base group's improvement portfolios.

In order for synergy to exist, everyone on the school's site transer team must carry out their specific responsibilities. The portfolios reflect accomplishments, and the accomplishments give evidence of commitment; but, commitments will vary. The organization shows its commitment by allocating time for information gathering, peer coaching, mentoring, and celebrations. Principals show commitment by encouraging risk taking and providing incentives for attention to application quality. Teachers show commitment by risking attempts at new ways of teaching.

Site transfer teams can function in a variety of ways. In addition to Joyce and Showers' (1983) peer-coaching model, best practices include action research teams, study groups, cognitive coaching teams, peer-assisted coaching teams, curriculum development teams, and quality circles.

Alignment of Learning Opportunities with School Vision

Traditional inservices are most noted as "fix 'em up" opportunities. Administrators decide what teachers need and schedule a motivational speaker to help them do a better job. Although this approach is preferable to inservice events with randomly chosen speakers, it falls short of a staff development program that has a committee which identifies teachers' wants and needs and then structures a response. It also fails to consider that professional development provides learning opportunities congruent with the school site's vision for improvement. In an approach that considers the teachers' concerns, the school community determines their mission and goals. Each faculty member or team can then frame their professional development to allow them to contribute to the common goals of the school community.

Assessing Professional Growth in the Transfer Paradigm

In light of schoolwide goals for improvement, individuals define personal improvement goals based on learning new ways to help children succeed. Personal improvement goals help individuals measure their contribution to the school's efforts toward better education.

Phi Delta Kappa's Center for Professional Development is piloting a model process for assessing performance and programs. Based on Glasser's (1986) control theory and the Costa-Garmston (1985) model of cognitive coaching, the "responsibility model of performance assessment" has three phases.

In phase one, the individual studies the school's improvement vision and goals, and then forms personal performance goals that align with the site's and district's goals. The individual then formulates a learning plan that provides the knowledge and skill necessary for carrying out the plan in the classroom. The sources of new knowledge may include workshops, courses, or seminars; books, discussion groups, videos, or Internet dialogues; training programs at the district office; or travel study. Finally, the individual decides what artifacts should go into a performance portfolio and what standards will be used to assess the study's results.

In phase two, the individual undertakes the study and applies his or her learning on the job. As the applications begin, the individual joins several colleagues in biweekly meetings to discuss how well the applications are working and what modifications are needed. Each application group sets its own interim performance standards and determines how group members will help each other meet these standards. In some cases, group members may agree to observe each other in the classroom and offer helpful suggestions.

In phase three, the individual organizes the portfolio according to the goals established in phase one. In addition to the group members, the individual invites his or her supervisor and two other people for a final review conference. In this conference, the individual exhibits the portfolio, reviews the original plan, and uses a rubric to show how well he or she instituted the desired changes, what modifications need to be made, and what assistance, if any, he or she needs from the conference committee. At this time, or later if desired by the principal, the individual develops a plan for the next year that either continues with refinements on the same course of study or embarks in a new direction.

In this responsibility model, the individual is the locus of control for professional assessment. There is an implicit assumption that more is gained in professional growth by facilitating internal motivation for learning and change through the development of personal goals aligned with the organization's goals than by the imposition of an "at command" model of teaching that is monitored by an annual supervisory visit, checklists, and a command performance.

There is also a second assumption, which aligns with the first. In this model, the supervisor's responsibility is not to evaluate but to coach. In addition to making time available for teams to peer coach, the administrator encourages each individual throughout the responsibility process. The administrator's primary function is to help each individual stay focused on the personal change plan. As part of the district's plan for professional development, the administrator should be given opportunities to include cognitive coaching in his or her professional growth plan.

Central to this process and integral to the success of any transfer-producing program of professional development is the concept of self-assessment. In addition to the individual's assessment of his or her professional development plan, school and district responsibility assessments are essential. Although legislators and staff offices of education may impose evaluation mechanisms, these mandates do not have to be counterproductive. More often than not, the mandates can provide a framework for district and individual improvement plans.

Consider this example: Esther Kennedy is a third-grade teacher in Illinois. Each year her third-grade students must take the Illinois Goal Assessment Program (IGAP) test as well as the California Test of Basic Skills (CTBS) mandated by her school board. In its approach to professional development, the district provided twenty hours of inservice, creating awareness of the Illinois State Board's vision, the IGAP, and the CTBS. The purpose of this program was to help each teacher see how these three external forces aligned with district goals. In these awareness sessions, the district presenter highlighted the state's number one priority—critical thinking—and discussed how the IGAP reading and math tests focused on critical thinking skills. Similarly, the presenter illustrated how the state vision called for mastery of basic skills and how the district would measure skill improvement through the CTBS.

Following the awareness session, Esther and the other third-grade teachers in her school constructed a group goal to review the reading and math curricula and the third-grade materials to see if they all aligned with the state and district goals for critical thinking. For their portfolio they gathered the artifacts of their discussions weighed against the alignment standard.

For the final conference, which included the principal, they were prepared to show what changes they wanted to make in curriculum and instruction and what they wanted to keep the same. They also noted *what* they needed to know more about and *how* they could get that information. Thus, from an awareness program conducted by the district with no cost for outside "experts," a professional development program emerged.

In these days of reform, many find it easy to scapegoat national, state, and district goals. As Glasser and others have taught, when a process is used that allows individuals in organizations to take personal responsibility for changes made, the scapegoating stops and individuals initiate constructive win-win change.

Opportunities to Observe and Confer
In addition to planning and assessing applications done in base groups, individuals have the option of inviting peers and/or administrators to observe applications being made in the classroom and to provide positive feedback. Constructive criticism is given only at the invitation of the teacher being observed. The site administrator is responsible for fulfilling requests to schedule these observations.

End-of-Year Exhibition
At the end of the school year, each base group prepares a public exhibition and/or a demonstration of the applications its members have refined. Other school teams, community members, and parents can attend and join the celebration.

End-of-Year Conference

Each individual meets with his or her supervisor at a year-end conference. Primary responsibility is placed on the individual to use the portfolio (Burke, Fogarty, & Belgrad, 1994) to demonstrate how he or she reached the personal improvement goals set earlier in the year using the schoolwide rubric.

Transfer Incentives

In current practice, incentives for continuing education are based on the old paradigm of acquiring information. When a teacher or principal finishes a course, a certificate program, or a degree program, the district awards either a step-and-scale pay increase or recertification points. When an inservice day is completed, inservice points are given. Time spent plus an A or a B on a knowledge test are the major criteria for any award. In the learning transfer paradigm, however, incentive is given for completed *application* of course knowledge. Not until teachers use a new concept or skill in their classroom are step-and-scale, career-ladder, or inservice points awarded.

The Transfer-Promoting Professional Development Program

Within the framework of the transfer-promoting organization, professional development opportunities at the school site work best if they align with the expectations of the school's transfer rubric. Within each professional development program, irrespective of length, medium, or topic, the following ingredients are important.

The Professional Development Learning Center

A room dedicated to professional development programs should provide an ample supply of training materials (newsprint, markers, a professional development library of print, software, media materials), equipment (overhead, giant screen, VCR, video projector for tape and computer, computer stations), and furniture (group work tables, materials display tables, computer stations, comfortable chairs) for group programs. It should also provide quiet study areas and technology stations for electronic access to information, Internet projects, teleconferencing, and project creation.

Posted Expectations for Transfer
Posting the school's vision, rubric, criteria for success, and schedules for base groups allows teachers, administrators, base groups, and mediators quick and easy access to program information. Visual reminders can be enhanced with letters from the district office or with videotaped statements by the superintendent or board president encouraging participation in the professional development program.

Display of Exemplary Applications
A bulletin board displaying photos of classroom applications, student artifacts, and end-of-year exhibitions not only communicates the importance of transfer from training, but also provides sample possibilities for those who appreciate "hands-on" models.

Visual Cues
Charts listing the coaching and mediating skills, problem-solving models, and collaborative guidelines can be displayed. These serve both to remind and to reinforce the expectation of the collaborative problem solving most helpful to the transfer process.

The Transfer-Focused Design of Learning
By establishing systemic norms for transfer, it becomes easier for individuals and teams to design programs that promote transfer. The systemic approach reduces the perceived barriers of time, curriculum coverage, low expectations of student performance, administrative support, peer support, and old paradigm understandings of inservice and "sit-and-get" staff development. However, it is important to remember that the systemic support groups that serve as the bedrock for high-transfer learning are but one side of the coin. The other side is the design of transfer-promoting ingredients within the learning program, be it a graduate course, seminar, workshop, or individual study.

Review of Expectations for Transfer

At the start of every training program, it is helpful to have an explicit reminder of the transfer purpose before and throughout the program. The trainer helps the participants switch focus from taking notes and covering the content to reflecting on the content for its application value. By calling attention to the expectation for transfer, the trainer reinforces the value of transfer. Finally, by taking time in the earliest sessions of the program to have participants set personal goals for transfer, the trainer encourages participants to take responsibility for their own learning and its application to their classrooms.

Individual study projects and team study groups provide a special challenge. In these cases, the participants can work with the principal, a team leader, or a professional development specialist to review the transfer expectation and to design suitable application goals.

Identifying Critical Concept and Method Elements

It is important that each learner be clear on the essential knowledge to be learned. In a training program, the trainer can mediate the participants' understanding of core concepts and critical attributes. This will facilitate the learners' ability to weed out ancillary information. Roger and David Johnson's (1986) identification of the five basic elements of cooperative learning—positive interaction, face-to-face interaction, individual accountability, interpersonal and small group skills, and group processing—and Fogarty and Bellanca's (1991) BUILD attributes of cognitive instruction are examples of this high-transfer identifying practice. (See Figure 9.)

Setting Goals for Transfer

In teams or alone, each individual beginning a new professional development task will frame goals for transferring the anticipated learning into the job responsibility.

Tactics for Enabling Transfer

The trainer or coach helps the learner achieve the transfer goals

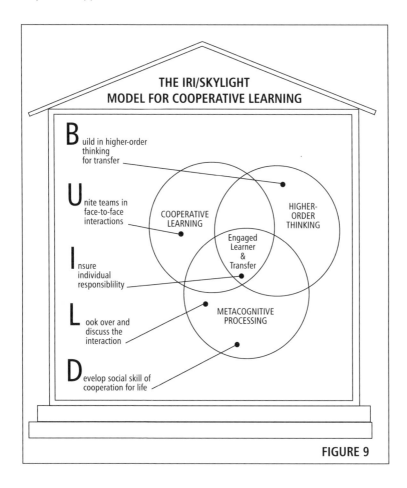

FIGURE 9

by employing tactics that encourage and enable transfer. For instance, in a training program, the trainer will make transfer "homework assignments" at the end of each session. At the start of the next session, the trainer will allow fifteen minutes for base groups to share the application artifacts resulting from the assignment. For example, the trainer in an Instrumental Enrichment program will ask each teacher to teach a lesson that applies mediative questioning. Each teacher will do this with students and tape-record his or her questions and the students' answers. In the base groups, each member will share the tape and invite feedback. After the groups have shared, the entire class will discuss common problems and seek out refinements.

Simulation of Best Practice

When possible, adult learners focused on transfer should engage in a simulation. It is important that the trainer model the use of a practice and engage participants in a simulated experience followed by an analysis of the practice. Then, participants have the opportunity to learn by doing. More importantly, if participants have no prior experience with the practice, the simulation provides them with a reference for designing applications with their own students.

When individuals and groups are engaged in self-directed study, it is helpful if they can design a practice demonstration for themselves. Observing a colleague using the practice with students or viewing video clips for analysis will help create a mental model.

Guided Application

After the mediated analysis of the practice, the trainer assigns participants to base teams of three to five members with similar content specialties or grade level assignments. Teams modify the observed practice for their students' needs and incorporate it into a lesson or unit. Where there are concerns about changing the curriculum, adult learners can work with familiar materials, including textbooks, as they redesign daily lessons to include the innovations.

Application Projects

Beyond lesson designs, team members produce classroom curriculum projects. These may include classroom learning centers, problem-based learning units, interdisciplinary "hands-on" projects with student materials, study kits, or other applications of ideas garnered in their study.

Application Reflection

In journals, adult learners take time to reflect

> "A past opportunity for me to use this practice in a lesson was . . ."
> "A lesson coming up which I could redesign is . . ."
> "A barrier to success for this practice is . . ."
> "A concern I have for using this practice is . . ."
> "A benefit of this practice for my students is . . . ."

Selective Abandonment

Simulations, guided applications, and reflections require different time schedules than lectures or workbook practice. As the trainer helps the participants integrate new practices into their daily schedule and abandon less important practices, participants' concerns about curriculum coverage become fewer, and they can focus more clearly on helping students understand key concepts.

Self-Assessment and Team Feedback on Transfer Goals

Using journals as well as team discussions, the trainer should encourage participants to focus on the quality of planned applications. When schedules allow staggered training sessions, participants can bring artifacts of their applications to the next training session and share the applications and the assessment of these artifacts with base groups. Positive feedback and support increase team bonding and problem solving. The stronger the bond created in the training program, the more successful the continuation of the base group after the training program's formal sessions end.

Continuous Encouragement

Leaving a familiar, comfortable way of teaching and beginning a new, foreign approach with different methods is a difficult challenge. Trainers, principals, coaches, and professional developers need to accentuate encouragement. Each time the adult learner expresses concern about using a new idea, it is important to respond: "You can do it!"

Barriers and Blocks to Problem Solving

Adult learners, well practiced in their response to a given set of job expectations, are seldom open to a new set of expectations for innovation. As Fullan points out, they tend to blow out of proportion the perceived and real barriers to implementation. Important tools for aiding the transfer process include discussions with peers who are overcoming barriers and problem-solving sessions specific to real and perceived barriers.

Applying Transfer in Professional Development Projects

The conflicting messages sent to schools about whether or not to change makes it difficult to move from staff development to professional development. It is even more difficult to make a *systemic* change. However, multischool projects are showing that such changes can produce high-transfer results.

Field-Based Master's Program for Teaching and Leadership

The Field-Based Master's Program (FBMP) is an innovative two-year graduate-degree program at St. Xavier University that boasts a 90 percent classroom application rate. This percentage contrasts with the long-established research that indicates little correlation between advanced degrees and teaching success. The FBMP program includes courses designed to utilize the transfer-promoting ingredients described above. It also includes team seminars in which base and cohort groups plan intensive applications of course content, analyze results, and reflect on the application process. Beginning with cooperative learning, each degree candidate creates a portfolio of student artifacts, journal entries, and mini-research projects. With each succeeding course built on the previous one, candidates create and evaluate their applications of critical thinking, performance assessment, curriculum integration, positive discipline, multiple intelligences, and problem-based learning. After fifteen months, base teams design action research projects to measure the success of their major implementations.

Each site team works with its principal to design and assess all applications and the action research project. Each candidate prepares a final public exhibition that demonstrates the success of the project. All projects are evaluated with preset performance standards—the most important being the degree to which the candidate has applied the material learned in the classroom. To date, three hundred graduates have not only demonstrated that learning transfer produced the desired changes in instruction, but also initiated school site changes with immeasurable results.

The Networks for Systemic Change

In 1992, IRI formed a partnership with Phi Delta Kappa to form The Network of Mindful Schools. Based on the success of that network in creating change within thirty schools, the organizations established two additional networks: The Multiple Intelligences School Network and the Total Quality in Education Network. As in the master's degree program, the design for change was made to include transfer-promoting ingredients.

In each network, a school leadership team works with the network coordinator and a consultant team to implement an annual tactical plan. Each organization's tactical plan aligns with the network's principles and the district's mission and goals for high achievement by all students. Six days per year, network consultants mediate the plan's staff development at the "how-to" level and facilitate the application of new knowledge and methods within the school's classrooms through peer team coaching, a site portfolio, and a community exhibition. School teams also gather for an annual conference.

In the network schools, principals and teachers employ strategic action planning as a key tool for enabling individual change as the cornerstone of organizational change. Understanding the need for a focused vision, these schools develop one that is shared by the other schools in that network: the mindful schools share the vision of intelligent behavior; the total quality schools work with Deming's fourteen principles; the multiple intelligences schools are centered around Gardner's theory. In the process of developing annual tactical plans, emphasis is placed on a practical vision. Each month in the network schools, a leadership team reviews the plan and marks progress. Each month the team considers whether or not the planned innovations, supported by the professional growth of the staff, are being used in the classrooms. When applications falter, the groups refrain from "blaming the teacher." Instead, they focus on what the barriers are and why they persist. They ask "What must we do to remove the barriers and accelerate the applications?" In this way, the team chips away at the old paradigm and creates systemic support for building the new.

New Launches in School Districts

Across the country, there are other emerging efforts to create systemic reform through professional development.

• In Milwaukee, Wisconsin, the city's middle schools have scheduled common periods for shared decision making and cooperative planning. Teams plan instructional goals, share expertise, discuss the successes of applications, and redesign instruction.

• In Greenville, Ohio, one school's teachers and principal meet weekly to plan and assess the implementation of cooperative learning strategies they are learning during six scheduled instruction days throughout the year. Breaking the isolation of the individual classroom, the first year's team sessions have lead to the resolution of other reform issues, involved the community in education, and transformed the school culture from a competitive to a collaborative workplace. In addition, the team made plans for revising curricula and integrating thinking skills.

• In Thompson, Georgia, an elementary school began its systemic reform journey with two teachers and a principal who wanted to implement whole language instruction schoolwide. After a faculty discussion, the implementation lead to the creation of study groups. Agreements to target reading improvement with the best researched methods sprang from these groups. Time was scheduled in the school day for grade-level teams to assess student needs and to develop action plans. With the school's limited budget, the faculty refrained from spending money for a consultant "expert" and established a plan for gathering new ideas from the district's library, for weekly peer-coaching team sessions that would allow ongoing action research on a schoolwide basis, and for an all-school celebration of their journey each month.

• In Illinois, the Association of Illinois Middle Schools (AIMS) has networked sixty-three schools to study the principles of systemic change and to plan site implementation. Each school is working on its own time line to establish theme teams that will develop innovations based on the systemic implementation of middle school philosophy. In the first three years, AIMS has facilitated the study teams and provided other staff development programs in response to the schools' identified needs. At the next level, twenty volunteer schools will design their own transfer-promoting systems for professional development and target instruction in science and math for improvement.

• In Durham, Ontario, the school system has used cooperative learning as the core of its development efforts. In the past five years, a development team has provided everything from introductions to application sessions, leadership training, and curriculum teams. The district is making cooperation an imperative in every classroom.

Creating an Environment Conducive to Learning Transfer

When a professional development opportunity is built on the assumption that the end comes with the final test of the information provided, or just ends, schools only hope that transfer "might" happen. However, experience with these outmoded beliefs tells us that transfer does not occur. Packed daily schedules, increased pressure to cover more content in less time, greater numbers of at-risk students in every classroom, and other issues make it very difficult for even the most dedicated and creative teachers to implement new ideas and new strategies. Like their adult counterparts in business and industry, teachers need assistance in transferring new ideas into specific, successful, on-the-job realities. Without a training environment that honors and celebrates transfer, transfer will not result.

In a professional development environment conducive to transfer, change does occur. Moreover, it happens in predictable stages over a period of time. Although there are no quick fixes, substantial changes that contribute to a vision of learning success for all children can be made by identifying goals, gathering information on possibilities for making the school site's vision a reality, and transfering theory into hands-on practice.

Bruce Williams (1993) outlines the process tactics that a skilled facilitator can use in guiding teams through stages of change:

1. Building the practical vision

2. Identifying action goals for the year

3. Selecting action tactics for the year

4. Dividing responsibilities and establishing timelines

5. Planning assessment points and making revisions

6. Renewing the cycle

Williams points out that this process works best when a person external to the group acts as the facilitator. This facilitator can be a district professional development coordinator, a principal or teacher from another building, or an external consultant. It is helpful if this facilitator is trained to guide the six-step process described above and to focus the group without interjecting his or her own ideas or manipulating the process to a preestablished end. The facilitator needs to have strong active listening skills, passive acceptance skills, the ability to clarify and summarize, the ability to manage conflict in a constructive manner, and a talent for moving the process forward to a common group goal. It is even more helpful if the facilitator is a trained and skilled user of such time-cutting, consensus-building strategies as cardstorming, graphic-thought organizers, data-analysis tactics, and assessment strategies. Finally, the facilitator should be able to guide the group through the processes with strong consensus-building strategies, and teach the methods to the group.

Making the Change

Change in professional development does not have to wait for the heavens to open with commands and mandates issued by a "higher authority." It is a basic principle of systemic change that any small modifications are enough to begin the change journey.

Usually, however, little thought is given to establishing transfer-promoting structures and strategies as a formal change component. Any school facility can begin the journey of systemic change by forming a leadership team to develop a tactical plan for ensuring professional, systemic development. As its first task, the team will assess the school's use of transfer-promoting strategies and structures. The following questionnaire will assist a team in its assessment.

ASSESSMENT OF PROFESSIONAL DEVELOPMENT

Step 1: System Assessment

Our staff may make use of the following options (check all that apply):

- ❏ one institute day per year for all
- ❏ several institute days per year, smorgasbord
- ❏ several institute days per year, single topic
- ❏ conference or seminar attendance
- ❏ graduate courses
- ❏ small-group team study
- ❏ independent study
- ❏ extended-day workshops on single topic
- ❏ other _____
- ❏ other _____

Teachers *use* these options:
    ❏ seldom   ❏ sometimes   ❏ 90%+

Administrators *use* these options:
    ❏ seldom   ❏ sometimes   ❏ 90%+

Options cover:	Yes	No
curricular content	❏	❏
teaching methods	❏	❏
classroom management	❏	❏
assessment_____	❏	❏
other _____	❏	❏

Incentives include:	Yes	No
step-and-scale points	❏	❏
released time	❏	❏
reimbursement	❏	❏
other _____	❏	❏

Incentives are provided for:	Yes	No
completion of a course or program	❏	❏
participation in peer-support or peer-coaching teams	❏	❏
portfolio of transfer evidence	❏	❏
exhibitions and celebrations	❏	❏

Transfer-promoting work environment factors used are:	Yes	No
posted and discussed explicit expectations for transfer	❏	❏
prescheduled base groups	❏	❏
prescheduled cohort groups	❏	❏
alignment of learning opportunities with school vision	❏	❏
transfer-based rubric for improvement	❏	❏
self-assessment procedures opportunities to confer	❏	❏
end-of-year conference based on individual application goals	❏	❏
end-of-year exhibits	❏	❏

Transfer-promoting professional development ingredients used are:	Yes	No
room set aside for professional development	❏	❏
posted expectations for transfer	❏	❏
posted transfer standards	❏	❏
displays of exemplary applications	❏	❏
visual cues	❏	❏

Transfer-promoting training design includes:	Yes	No
review of transfer expectation prior to each learning event	❏	❏
identification of key concepts in learning event	❏	❏
setting of goals for transfer	❏	❏
tactics for enabling transfer	❏	❏
simulation of best practice	❏	❏
guided application	❏	❏
application reflections	❏	❏
selective abandonment encouragement	❏	❏
self-assessment and team feedback for transfer goals	❏	❏
continuous encouragement	❏	❏
schedule of review of applications with celebrations	❏	❏
problem solving for barriers to application	❏	❏

Step 2: Data Analysis

Under "helpers," list ten practices your organization uses that contribute to a strong professional development program. Under "drawbacks," list ten practices that are missing or are not functioning properly.

Helpers	Drawbacks

1. Rate the "helpers" from 1 to 10.
   (1 = weakest, 10 = strongest). You may use the same rating several times. For example, several practices could be rated 8.

2. Repeat the ratings for the "drawbacks."
   (1 = nonexistent, 10 = chance for improvement).

3. Plan for change. Take three helpers that could be strengthened and three drawbacks that have potential for becoming helpers and make a plan.

4. For each of the six items above, make a goal sheet with a measurable goal for change. List barriers, strategies for achieving the goal, responsibilities, and time lines; then make an assessment.

Step 3: Implementation Plan

Goal for implementing transfer

_____
_____
_____
_____

Barriers to transfer (excluding time and money)

_____
_____
_____
_____

Structures and strategies to promote transfer

_____
_____
_____
_____

Responsibilities (Who?)

_____
_____
_____
_____

Deadlines

_____
_____
_____
_____

Assessment of goal

_____
_____
_____
_____

Taking Charge of Change

After the school leadership team completes its professional development change plan, it is time to decide on tactical steps. This may begin with a cardstorming session. In this session the team will identify all the tasks that must be done in order to achieve its transfer-promoting goals. As described by R. Bruce Williams (1993), cardstorming is most effective when a facilitator guides the team through the process. The facilitator may be a principal, a teacher, a staff developer, or a community member. For the cardstorming process, the facilitator needs a large wall space, a pile of five-by-seven-inch index cards, tape, and a dozen markers.

To begin, one member of the team tapes seven cards, each with a different symbol (see below for an example), to the wall.

Then the facilitator poses the launch question to the group: What are all the transfer-promoting tasks that must be completed to accomplish the change goals? Next, the facilitator guides the team members, working in pairs or alone, through these steps:

1. Using 8–10 index cards, participants write one idea per card (see below for an example), limiting each description to 4–5 words.

> SCHEDULE
> CLASSROOM
> OBSERVATIONS

2. After a predetermined period of time, participants rank their cards in order from the most important to the least important.

3. The facilitator then asks for one card from each person, or small group, and tapes each to the wall under one of the symbol-marked cards. Team members should all agree on which column each card should be placed as it is presented.

4. After all the cards have been placed in columns, the team gives a name to each column according to its common factor. The facilitator writes each column name on a separate card and replaces the symbol cards with the new names. An example follows.

Making Transfer Expectations Clear	Designing Training Events for Transfer	Developing Base Group Plans	Highlighting Transfer Elements	Structuring Projects	Promoting Transfer Metacognition	Assessing Transfer

5. Then the team sequences the cards in each column in a sequence chart. For example, a sequence chart for "Developing Base Group Plans" might look like this:

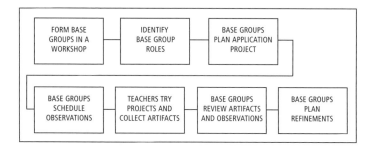

6. After all the cards are sequenced, the team agrees on time lines, responsibilities, and assessment of the transfer-promoting goal.

Following the cardstorming process, one team member will be designated as the "checker" to periodically check the progress of the transfer-promoting tasks in the school's professional development plan and to monitor the implementation of transfer-promoting strategies. The implementation stage is the most difficult to get through. Spontaneous interruptions, regular day-to-day tasks, and other barriers make implementation difficult and distract schools from their focus. Through one-to-one encouragement, review meetings, special notes, site newsletters, and other communication tools, the facilitator helps the school stay on the course of change and avoid discouragement when first implementations are not perfect. Team problem-resolution sessions, data gathering, feedback on individual and team accomplishments, and teamwork sessions to celebrate transfer successes energize the team members to overcome individual frustrations and help them remember that the change project is a team effort.

Assessing the Results

The most important results in a school's change effort are found in the effect on student learning. Measuring the effect is essential, but not until the changes in the system have been assessed. By assessing targeted changes, the school team will be able to gather data on how well the program is being implemented schoolwide. For instance, is there a coaching schedule in place? Do the teachers take advantage of it? Are they transferring learning into their classrooms? How is the transfer being shown?

To assess how well the school site is promoting transfer, the team can reuse the survey on pages 51–55 to evaluate observable transfer-promoting strategies. If the school already has these strategies in place, the team can create a rubric that measures the quality of transfer or the increase in transfer.

As the team collects evidence of the program implementation and the effectiveness of the transfer-promoting strategies, it builds a school assessment portfolio and, eventually, an exhibition. The exhibit shows the public how the school has used a collaborative effort to bring constructive change through professional development.

The Paradigm Shift

At the end of a semester or a school year, the school leadership team has the opportunity to look back and review the portfolio of individual and schoolwide accomplishments. Noting what it did well in establishing transfer-promoting strategies, deciding how it will make adjustments, and investigating new directions, the team progresses in the systemic change process. The end of one goal flows into the beginning of a new goal which will better insure that individual and organizational development walk the same path (Fullan, 1991). Looking at the transfer-promoting practice it has instituted, the team will see a major paradigm shift that will have a long-term impact on every project it develops in future years.

PROFESSIONAL DEVELOPMENT: CHANGING TIMES

ASSUMPTIONS DRIVING INSERVICE PROGRAMS	ASSUMPTIONS DRIVING PROFESSIONAL DEVELOPMENT
• Periodic inservice days are sufficient to introduce teachers to new ideas and to improve practice.	• Ongoing professional development is required if it is to result in significant change.
• Professional development should improve and remediate individual teaching practice.	• School change is the result of both individual and organizational development.
• The goal of professional development is to transfer knowledge and discrete skills from "experts" to teachers.	• The goal of professional development is to support the inquiry into and study of teaching and learning.
• The most effective way for teachers to learn is for them to listen to a speaker.	• Teachers learn as a result of training, practice, and feedback, as well as individual reflection and group inquiry into their practice.
• Professional development is more of a luxury than an essential element of a district's educational program.	• Professional development is essential to school development.
• "Pull-out" training at the district level is the most effective delivery mode.	• Professional development should be primarily school focused and embedded in the job.

From Carole Fine, with Lenaya Raack, "Professional Development: Changing Times" (*Policy Briefs*, Report 4, 1994), p. 2. Copyright © 1994, North Central Regional Educational Laboratory. Reprinted with permission.

These are changing times (Fine, 1994). At no other time in history have the demands for change so pressured schools. However, it is easier to talk theoretically about what schools *ought* to do, than it is to institutionalize the desired changes. Educators must take charge and control change in productive ways. Now is the time to begin the change journey—the journey from outdated practices toward the goal of systemic change through professional development.

Bibliography

Ben-Hur, M. (Ed.). (1994). *On Feuerstein's Instrumental Enrichment: A collection.* Palatine, IL: IRI/Skylight Publishing.

Burke, K. (1994). *How to assess authentic learning.* Palatine, IL: IRI/Skylight Publishing.

Burke, K., Fogarty, R., & Belgrad, S. (1994). *The mindful school: The portfolio connection.* Palatine, IL: IRI/Skylight Publishing.

Cohen, A. (1993, June). A new educational paradigm. *Phi Delta Kappan,* pp. 791–795.

Costa, A. L. (1991). *The school as a home for the mind.* Palatine, IL: IRI/Skylight Publishing.

Costa, A. L., Bellanca, J., & Fogarty, R. (Eds.). (1992). *If minds matter: A foreword to the future* (Vol. 2). Palatine, IL: IRI/Skylight Publishing.

Costa, A. L., & Garmston, R. (1985, February). Supervision for intelligent teaching. *Educational Leadership,* pp. 70, 72–80.

Deming, E. (1986). *Out of the crisis.* Cambridge, MA: MIT Center for Advanced Engineering Study.

Donahoe, T. (1993, December). Finding the way: Structure, time and culture in school improvement. *Phi Delta Kappan,* pp. 298–305.

Everson, C. M. (1994). *Classroom management for elementary teachers.* Needham Heights, MA: Allyn & Bacon.

Feuerstein, R. (1980). *Instrumental Enrichment.* Baltimore, MD: University Park Press.

Fine, C., with Raack, L. (1994). Professional development: Changing times. *Policy Briefs,* Report 4, 2–6.

Fogarty, R. (1994). *The mindful school: How to teach for metacognitive reflection.* Palatine, IL: IRI/Skylight Publishing.

Fogarty, R. (1989). *From training to transfer: The role of creativity in the adult learner.* Doctoral dissertation, Loyola University of Chicago, Illinois.

Fogarty, R., & Bellanca, J. (1991). *Patterns for thinking—Patterns for transfer.* Palatine, IL: IRI/Skylight Publishing.

Fogarty, R., Perkins, D., & Barell, J. (1992). *The mindful school: How to teach for transfer.* Palatine, IL: IRI/Skylight Publishing.

Fuhrman, S. H. (1994). Challenges in systemic education reform. *CPRE Policy Briefs,* 1–7.

Fullan, M. (1993). *Change forces: Probing the depths of educational reform.* London: The Falmer Press.

Fullan, M. G. (1991). *The new meaning of educational change.* New York: Teachers College Press.

Gardner, H., & Boix-Mansilla, V. (1994, February). Teaching for understanding—Within and across disciplines. *Educational Leadership,* pp. 14–18.

Gardner, H. (1983). *Frames of mind: The theory of multiple intelligences.* New York: Basic Books.

Garmston, R., Linder, C., & Whitaker, J. (1993, October). Reflections of cognitive coaching. *Educational Leadership,* pp. 57–61.

Glasser, W. (1986). *Control theory in the classroom.* New York: Harper.

Goodlad, J. I. (1994). *Educational renewal: Better teachers, better schools.* San Francisco: Jossey-Bass.

Goodlad, J. I. (1994, April). The national network for educational renewal. *Phi Delta Kappan,* pp. 632–638.

Goodlad, J. I. (1991, November). Why we need a complete redesign of teacher education. *Educational Leadership,* pp. 4–6, 8–10.

Goodlad, J. I. (1990, November). Better teachers for our nation's schools. *Phi Delta Kappan,* pp. 184–194.
Hitt, W. (1994). *The leader-manager.* Columbus, OH: Battelle Press.
Hunter, M. (1984). Knowing, teaching, and supervising. In P. L. Hosford (Ed.), *Using what we know about teaching* (pp. 169–203). Alexandria, VA: Association for Supervision and Curriculum Development.
Johnson, D. W., & Johnson, R. (1986). *Circles of learning: Cooperation in the classroom.* Alexandria, VA: Association for Supervision and Curriculum Development.
Joyce, B. R. (1986). *Improving America's schools.* New York: Longman.
Joyce, B. R., & Showers, B. (1988). *Student achievement through staff development.* New York: Longman.
Joyce, B. R., & Showers, B. (1983). *Power in staff development through research and training.* Alexandria, VA: Association for Supervision and Curriculum Development.
Kerman, Sam. (1979, June). Teacher expectations and student achievement: "Why did you call on me? I didn't have my hand up!" *Phi Delta Kappan,* pp. 716–718.
Knowles, M. S. (1983, Fall). Adults are not grown-up children as learners. *Community Services Catalyst,* pp. 4–8.
Knowles, M. S. (1975). *Self-directed learning: A guide for learners and teachers.* New York: Cambridge, The Adult Education Co.
Lieberman, A., & McLaughlin, M. W. (1992, May). Networks for educational change: Powerful and problematic. *Phi Delta Kappan,* pp. 673–677.
Little, J. W. (1993, Summer). Teacher professional development in a climate of educational reform. *Educational Evaluation and Policy Analysis,* pp. 129–151.
McCarthy, B. (1985, April). What 4MAT training teaches us about staff development. *Educational Leadership,* pp. 61–68.
McLaughlin, M. W. (1993). What matters most in teachers' workplace content? In J. W. Little & M. W. McLaughlin (Eds.), *Teachers work: Individuals, colleagues, and contexts* (pp. 79–103). New York: Teachers College Press.
National Education Commission on Time and Learning. (1994). *Prisoners of time.* Washington, DC: U.S. Government Printing Office.
O'Day, J., & Smith, M. S. (1993). Systemic school reform and educational opportunity. In S. H. Fuhrman (Ed.), *Designing coherent education policy: Improving the system* (pp. 313–322). San Francisco: Jossey-Bass.
Oxman, W. G., & Barell, J. (1983, April 11–15). *Reflective thinking in schools: A survey of teacher perceptions.* Paper presented at the 67th Annual Meeting of the American Educational Research Association, Montreal, Quebec.
Palincsar, A. S., & Brown, A. L. (1986, March). *Guided, cooperative learning and individual knowledge acquisition.* (Technical Report No. 372). Cambridge, MA: Bolt, Beranek & Newman, and Urbana, IL: Illinois University, Center for the Study of Reading. (ERIC Document Reproduction Service No. ED 270 738)
Perkins, D., & Salomon, G. (1988, September). Teaching for transfer. *Educational Leadership,* pp. 22–32.
Piaget, J. (1972). *The psychology of intelligence.* Totowa, NJ: Littlefield Adams.
Raywid, M. A. (1993, September). Finding time for collaboration. *Educational Leadership,* pp. 30–34.
Sarason, S. B. (1990). *The predictable failure of educational reform: Can we change course before it's too late?* San Francisco: Jossey-Bass.
Senge, P. (1990). *The fifth discipline: The art and practice of the learning organization.* New York: Doubleday.
Showers, B. (1984). *Transfer of training: The contribution of coaching.* Eugene, OR: Center for Educational Policy and Management.

Slavin, R. E. (1991, February). Synthesis of research on cooperative learning. *Educational Leadership*, pp. 71–82.

Smith, M. S., & O'Day, J. (1991). Systemic school reform. In S. Fuhrman & B. Malen (Eds.), *The politics of curriculum and testing*, (pp. 233–267). Bristol, PA: Falmer Press.

Thorndike, E. L. (1969). *Educational psychology*. New York: Arno Press.

Vygotsky, L. S. (1978). *Mind in society: The development of higher psychological processes*. Edited by M. Cole, V. John-Steiner, S. Scribner, & E. Souberman. Cambridge, MA: Harvard University Press.

Williams, R. B. (1993). *More than 50 ways to build team consensus*. Palatine, IL: IRI/ Skylight Publishing.

Williams, J. R., & Kopp, W. L. (1994). Implementation of Instrumental Enrichment and cognitive modifiability in the Taunton public schools: A model for systemic implementation in U.S. schools. In M. Ben-Hur (Ed.), *On Feuerstein's Instrumental Enrichment: A collection* (pp. 261–272). Palatine, IL: IRI/Skylight Publishing.

Winograd, P., Turner, T., & McCall, A. (1990, November 27–December 1). *Influential teachers and receptive students*. Paper presented at the 40th Annual Meeting of the National Reading Conference, Miami, Florida.

Wlodkowski, R. J. (1985, November). How to plan motivational strategies for adult instruction. *Performance and Instruction*, pp. 1–6.

There are
one-story intellects,
two-story intellects, and three-story
intellects with skylights. All fact collectors, who have
no aim beyond their facts, are one-story men. Two-story men compare,
reason, generalize, using the labors of the fact collectors as well as their
own. Three-story men idealize, imagine, predict—
their best illumination comes from
above, through the skylight.

—Oliver Wendell
Holmes